Secrets I Learned
From Ordinary House Cats

Wit and Wisdom for Life!

Rosemary Augustine

Secrets I Learned From Ordinary House Cats

Rosemary Augustine

Published by:

Blue Spruce Publishing Company

2175 Golf Isle Drive, Suite 1024

Melbourne, FL 32935

610.647.8863

info@BlueSprucePublishing.com

Cover Photo: Dave and Buster by Flora McCarty
Author Photo: Billy Tave
Ziggy and Zack Photos: Rosemary Augustine

Cat Graphics provided by OpenClipArt.org

Copyright © 2013, 2016 - Rosemary Augustine

All rights reserved.

ISBN-10: 0-9644711-4-0
ISBN-13: 978-09644711-4-6

DEDICATION

I dedicate this book to all the kitty lovers of the world. And especially those who rescue feral kittens.

There is a wealth of dedication to animals in general and especially cats that make these rescue individuals valuable to the human race.

A heartfelt thank you to the veterinarians, veterinarian technicians, animal shelters, office staff, pet sitters and animal lovers who make felines a priority in their lives.

And a BIG Thank You to Dr. Rowan and Gina DeMarco for changing my life with these two cats. Thank You from the bottom of my heart!

CONTENTS

Chapter 1 - No Ordinary Love	1
Chapter 2 - Listen For Predators	5
Chapter 3 - Observation Deck	9
Chapter 4 - Eye For Detail	15
Chapter 5 - Competition	21
Chapter 6 - Give Your Best	27
Chapter 7 - Flexibility	33
Chapter 8 - Exhibit Poise	39
Chapter 9 - Laughter	43
Chapter 10 - Humor	49
Chapter 11 - Uncertainty	53
Chapter 12 - Share	59
Chapter 13 - Be in the Moment	65
Chapter 14 - A Defining Moment	69

A Word From the Author...
About Ziggy and Zack

Six kittens were born to a feral momma cat somewhere near Berwyn, PA in the spring of 2005. Not long after the momma moved her six kittens to a safer location, she was found dead in the road... leaving behind her 5-week old kittens. Fortunately, my local vet, Dr. Rowan of Paoli Vet Care, was familiar with the momma, so one of his vet techs rescued the kittens.

In no time, my pet sitter, Gina DeMarco, having learned about these orphaned kittens, called me to inquire if I was ready for a new cat after my last two had recently died. To her surprise I was, and I was looking for two kittens.

On an afternoon in late May of that year, I visited Paoli Vet Care to view these orphaned kittens. Much to my surprise, I was instantly smitten with one feisty black kitten and the quieter striped one. Within an hour, I returned home with two males - a grey striped tabby and a black and white tuxedo ... later that night to be named Ziggy and Zack.

It goes without saying, these two felines made a difference to me at a very significant time in my life. Instantly we bonded as family. However, as kittens, these two felines were quite a handful and at three months old, taught me tricks about life that gave me instant pause. It all began with watching Ziggy open the screen door, as he had seen me do so many times.

After losing two other felines, my beloved Byron of 18+ years and my little Maxx of 13 years – both within 18 months of each other - jump-starting a new kitty family, especially with two kittens made me hesitate - if only for a moment. However, within a few weeks, Ziggy and Zack brought a new dimension to the Augustine household.

As kittens, they both quickly won the hearts of me and the residents of Berwyn. They loved the outdoors and feared no one. They took command of the 2nd story balcony and made sure no one entered our home without approval. And it goes without saying, they loved flower pots!

Let me introduce you to a gray-striped tabby named Ziggy, and a black and white tuxedo cat named Zack. Between the two of them, in just a matter of a few months, they demonstrated a talent that translated into valuable life skills for humans in our everyday living.

As a result, I looked at life from a very different perspective while watching ordinary kittens change into adult cats. I created this book of *wit and wisdom for life*, as their life unfolded before my very eyes. It took my breath away, and in the end, I decided to reveal their "secrets."

I'm not sure that these two kitties know of the deep inspiration they continue to provide me. However, I only hope they know and understand how much they are loved and how much joy they bring me every day.

1

No Ordinary Love

Rosemary Augustine

"Experience the power of unconditional love."

Secrets I Learned From Ordinary House Cats

First let me say ...

No cat is ordinary!

And if you don't like cats,

You probably will after reading this book.

Just when you wonder

What are they up to now?

Ziggy and Zack have a way,

Of winning your heart,

And making you smile.

They will make you crazy

With their silly antics, daring feats...

And oh,

Their quiet presence...

However...

They command attention

Of many sorts!

Never underestimate

The reach of a cat...

How far they can jump...

And...

How much they can love.

2

Listen for Predators

Rosemary Augustine

"Words can either lift up or destroy."

Negative thinking destroys all senses...

Eventually.

In a negative world,

Finding a glimmer

of positive thoughts, words or deeds

IS challenging.

Create

a positive environment

Of ...

What you say, think, and hear,

And you will open

New and different

Doors to explore.

Listen! Can you hear?

I can hear even when ...

There is no sound.

Long before others wince at the noise...

I hear danger in the night

And love at sunrise...

I hear my breath ...

During a long hot summer daze...

I listen intently for negative sounds ...

And deflect with my positive shield of peace...

Predators are dangerous

For they feed on negativity,

And want to draw me into their dark world.

As I listen for predators ...

I am strong with the light ... and the power

of positive words.

3

Observation Deck

Rosemary Augustine

"Always be curious."

Secrets I Learned From Ordinary House Cats

From this vantage point

You have the opportunity

To watch, learn and do,

Then repeat to learn ...

New skills.

 I watch you – daily,

And with my eyes

I observe life.

I take notice

Watching people ... animals ...

The world ... It's fascinating

Since sometimes you have no clue

That I'm watching you...

And then ...

If our eyes meet,

You quickly look away,

Feeling guilty because ...

I caught you watching me.

Secrets I Learned From Ordinary House Cats

My observation deck

Is a vantage point

And my opportunity

To watch, learn and grow.

I'm curious.

I want to see and do

As much as I can

with my life.

My days and nights

Are filled ...

With wonderment

Of observing

All that my mind

and eyes can see.

Rosemary Augustine

4

Eye for Detail

Rosemary Augustine

"See the big picture ...

and also know how to handle the details."

Secrets I Learned From Ordinary House Cats

Whether being neat and organized

when awake,

Or sound asleep dreaming,

Always keep one eye open.

Watch,

And make sure ...

All the details of life are covered.

I am known

For my fastidious ways,

Don't let me fool you.

It is important

To be neat and organized

When my eyes are open.

And wander lazily

Through my dreams when sleeping.

Secrets I Learned From Ordinary House Cats

The key to detail

Is still being able to

See the big picture ...

When I'm awake ...

Asleep ...

Or deep in the muck of things.

And to remember,

The prize may only be

Just a few feet away...

Not quite arms reach.

But it is what's

around me...

Below me ...

Above me ...

and all around me

That I need to keep in mind

As I reach out ...

and risk life and limb.

5

Competition

Rosemary Augustine

"Competition gives way to choice."

Secrets I Learned From Ordinary House Cats

Smell your competition

And smell them miles away

Since you may find that

Some days you eat the competition ...

and other days ...

You play with them.

Competition is healthy.

It gives choice...

It gives opportunity...

It gives grace.

You can be afraid of your competition,

You can join them

Or you can beat them at their own game.

However, there are times

You will sit across the table

From your competition

And join in a meal,

Maybe even conversation...

It is at this time

You become colleagues rather than competitors.

And by joining forces,

Great things can be accomplished...

by building a strategic alliance

with your so called "competition."

And on those days

When others

Are being eaten alive...

You will have joined forces

With the competition ...

 And you will find strength

in numbers.

Rosemary Augustine

6

Give Your Best

"Stir up a whirlwind of why you're the best!"

Simply put ...

Every day

Is a Great Day!

Today I feel blah!

But...

I know

What I need to get done

And how important it is

To the greater scheme of things.

So although I feel blah,

I'm going to give my best...

My best as if it is a great day ...

And I'm on top of the world...

Even though

Secretly I'm not ...

Every day is a great day...

Regardless of how I feel.

So... I'm going to be present

In the moment

And savor every moment...

Because once it's over...

I can never live that moment again.

Secrets I Learned From Ordinary House Cats

It is important

To be my best,

Not for you,

But for me...

Because I matter!

And I value my presence ...

Here on earth ...

Everyday...

Because...

Every day is a Great Day!

Rosemary Augustine

7

Flexibility

"Flexibility is a key component to life!"

Secrets I Learned From Ordinary House Cats

You definitely want to be flexible

For those days when...

You need to bend over backwards

Or for the moments when ...

You need to jump hoops.

Today I'm jumping hoops...

Trying to please

Everyone else.

I never knew

How important

Flexibility was

Until ...

I had to exercise it ...

Multiple times a day.

How important for me

To exercise flexibility

With both my mind and body...

So I can jump hoops...

Flex backward...

Run...

Or walk ...

At the demands of life.

If I am flexible,

I can move

With the ebb

and flow of life ...

And not worry

About stepping on someone else's toes ...

Because if I'm flexible

I will have the finesse

Of flying through the air ...

With the greatest of ease...

At times when others ...

Are falling off the trapeze.

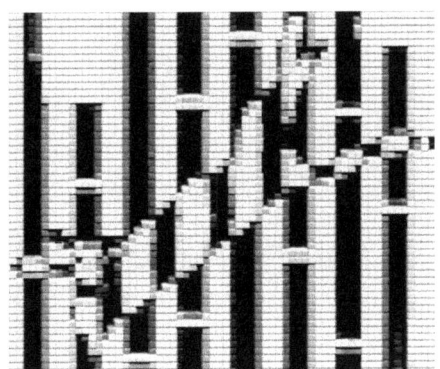

Rosemary Augustine

8

Exhibit Poise

"Walk through your fear."

Display poise

When you need

To demonstrate

Diplomacy ...

And confidence ...

As well as

Extending gratitude

for the day.

I wait ...

Patiently

No longer fearful of abandon.

As you prepare dinner ...

I am humbled

Rosemary Augustine

By us sharing... and

Grateful that

You came into my life.

9

Laughter

"Laughter lightens the heart and lifts the soul."

Secrets I Learned From Ordinary House Cats

Never does a day pass

I don't make you laugh.

Your smile,

And the sound of your laughter

Makes you happy ...

And downright silly looking.

Laughter is medicine

For the mind, body and soul...

Without laughter,

Life would not be the same.

There would be too much silence...

Life would not be alive

There would be no fun...

No joy...

No happiness...

In other words...

I'm glad I make you laugh.

Laugh regularly

Throughout the day

And know the lines

on your face ...

Are from laughing loudly,

Deep-in-the-belly laughter, with tears rolling down your face...

Goofy, crazy, silly, laughter - daily!

Just make sure …

You laugh at yourself …

And not laugh at others.

And know with laughter …

Comes joy in your soul.

10

Humor

"Stress can and will ultimately kill you."

Secrets I Learned From Ordinary House Cats

Lighten up

And don't take life so seriously.

Have a sense of humor.

And realize that ...

Humor gives laughter it's sound.

Find the humor

In as much as you can

As often as you can

Throughout the day.

And you will find

You just may have

More smiles

And a lot less stress.

Rosemary Augustine

11

Uncertainty

Rosemary Augustine

"You are a pioneer ...

driving where there are no roads."

For those moments

When all else fails?

Look at life

From a different perspective...

And ask...

"What would Ziggy do?"

I hope by now ...

You know the answer!

Rosemary Augustine

And Lastly...

Rosemary Augustine

12

Share

"Look deep inside ... and only then...

you can find the true meaning of life."

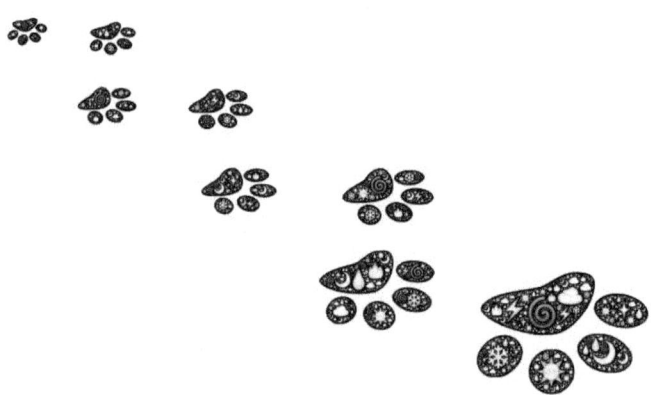

Unconditionally share

Your love...

And your life.

However...

Ziggy never

shares his food

Since...

food gives him strength

For the days

he eats the competition,

Tackles that new skill

And follows up on details.

You, however,

Will need to work at staying positive ...

And succeed at all you do...

While having poise ...

Flexibility ...

And a sense of humor...

Secrets I Learned From Ordinary House Cats

As you ...

Listen for predators...

Have an eye for detail...

While you sit on your observation deck...

Smelling the competition.

And also remember...

Find a reason to laugh

at yourself...

So you can

not only be your best...

But give your best

to the world...

Every day!

13

Be In the Moment

"Forget what's past and stop worrying about what might be... learn to be "in the moment."

Secrets I Learned From Ordinary House Cats

To be in the moment

forsakes the past and future.

It simply means ... Now!

I am in the moment when my eyes are affixed on my prey.

I am in the moment when I am sharing life with my precious human.

I am in the moment at my food bowl ...

or the litter box.

I don't worry about what is past

And I don't fret about what is to come.

I enjoy the sunshine when its warm rays soak my body.

I don't worry about whether the sun will shine tomorrow for I only care about now.

And when tomorrow comes,

I will enjoy the sunshine again

As if it was for the first time.

I am filled with the moment,

And fulfilled with the thought of it.

14

A Defining Moment

"When you realize what's really important in life, nothing else matters."

Secrets I Learned From Ordinary House Cats

Rosemary Augustine

My defining moment is when ...

I know I wont always be here.

I know someday I'll be gone ...

And I know it's not in my power,

No matter how much I want to stay.

But for now, let's not linger or worry

About future unknowns.

Let's be with one another in the moment.

Share in the joy of life as we know it now.

Revel in the beauty of our surroundings.

And, when I'm gone, let your memories of me fill those dark moments ...

And put a smile on your face that I was and always will be ... the love of your life!

Rosemary Augustine

About Zack

as told by the author

Zack was a fiesty kitten and even fiestier as an adult male cat. He ruled and he let Ziggy know it. It was often thought that Zack was the lead cat, because of his aggressive nature with his more laid back brother, Ziggy. Zack would instigate play and roughhouse with Ziggy. Often Zack would straddle Ziggy and bite him until you heard cat screams. However, many mornings clumps of black fur were often found where it was obvious that Ziggy got back at him. They were brothers, but they were complete opposites.

Coming from a rough beginning, he felt abandoned by his momma cat at 4 weeks old. Some say he may have witnessed her death. As a result, he demonstrated the need for constant love and attention. Zack grew into a quiet, reserved adult cat, and became a lap cat once he was out of his kitten stage. Extremely curious, what ever was on the floor was soon in his mouth. He loved people and loved watching people walk by the path our home overlooked. He was open to being petted by strangers, which was odd for a cat with a ferol background.

Zack was always seeking attention with his cute poses even when he was asleep. He especially liked to roll on his back so you could rub his belly - even by strangers once he approved of them. When I was first introduced to the tuxedo kitten, he hissed and spat with claws extended as I held him by the scruff of the neck and looked at him eye to eye. I then took the hissing/spatting kitten and tucked him under my chin, where he quickly began to purr and fell asleep. "I'll take this one for sure" was my response.

Zack enjoyed the 2nd floor patio at Main Line Berwyn Apartments in Berwyn, PA, often walking the patio railing the first 8 years of his life. He was excited making chirping sounds when the birds were at the feeder just outside the window. And Zack was a champion in catching bugs - his favorite was the summer cicadas that would nest in the surrounding trees. He would catch them in mid air, and share them with his big brother Ziggy. It was nature at work watching him during this bug decimation. And, in his lifetime, Zack caught a rat... a big one that hung from his mouth to the floor. He was thrilled to show me and then he released it to safety, somehow knowing it would totally escape.

When we moved to a new apartment on the opposite side of the building in the summer of 2013, the move was stressful for Zack (we moved all of 52 steps down the hall). Eventually he enjoyed the patio, this time overlooking the sidewalk where he watch neighbors come and go. Once we moved, he never jumped up on the railing again. When my mom moved in a few weeks later, Zack was instrumental in "showing her the way" as she used her walker up and down the hallway. He would often spend time with her in her room, keeping her company throughout the day. She called him Blackie.

Zack suddenly took ill in October, 2014, and was laid to rest on Wednesday, October 8, 2014 after being hospitalized briefly and diagnosed with advanced stages of Congestive Heart Failure and elevated

Kidney functions. The last 20 hours of his life he spent in an oxygen tank to assist with his breathing. Zack was just 9 years old. His death was a shock to me because it was so sudden. I recall his spirit appearing to me right after he died. I asked why he had to go so young? His response that I heard was: "I finished what I came here to do." The spiritual person that I am accepts this even though I don't fully understand.

Zack is sadly missed by me - his life-long human companion, and his litter mate and brother Ziggy, all the birds and squirrels of Main Line Berwyn Apartments, and many friends and neighbors. He is resting peacefully with other deceased feline companions of mine including Byron and Maxx, and my mother who died four months prior to Zack. Zack's ashes are now included on the kitty memorial shelf along with Byron (1985-2003) and Maxx 1992-2005).

Zack is fondly remembered as the feline duo of Ziggy and Zack in the book *"Secrets I Learned From Ordinary House Cats."* Thoughts and memories are part of my journaling practice to help ease the pain of his loss. May he always be remembered. RIP Zack!

Secrets I Learned From Ordinary House Cats

...

Zack in 2013

Rosemary Augustine

ABOUT ZIGGY

as told by the author

A shy but curious kitten, Ziggy grew into being a very shy adult cat. People would visit our home and he would never make an appearance. One visitor said, "If I didn't see the litter box in the bathroom, I wouldn't know you have a cat." Pet sitter after pet sitter would never see Ziggy while caring for him in my absence. Except one... Sheila. Ziggy hissed and growled at her for a week. He has yet to warm up to anyone who comes into the Augustine home.

Ziggy followed Zack's lead when they were young as they were always together, finding trouble, catching prey and sharing it. Though when Zack caught the rat, he did not share it. Often Ziggy and Zack were curled up together, whether on the bed or on the patio. They were two peas in a pod. As kittens they were in all kinds of trouble. As adults, they continued to jump the patio railing and just sit, balancing as they watched the world go by. It was nerve wracking watching them balance on the two inch wide railing. Never once did they fall or try to jump off.

We moved in the summer of 2013 to an apartment down the hall, to accommodate my aging mother. As the sea of people in and out began on a daily basis to care for my mother, Ziggy hid under the bed or under the covers. He wanted no part of strangers trying to befriend him. He never went into my mother's room unless I was in there. And only then did he sit right by the entrance watching us - ready to make a quick exit. However, the night my mother died, Ziggy was found sleeping on her robe. Somehow, he knew she was gone.

Ziggy watched curiously as I transformed my mother's bedroom into my art studio. But four months later, when Zack suddenly died, Ziggy was thrown into a whirlwind of abandonment that he didn't exhibit when he was a kitten losing his cat momma. He didn't understand why everyone was leaving and never coming back. And I sensed he feared losing me, since he became very close to me never wanting me to leave his side.

Since I was planning relocation in the spring of 2015 to another state a thousand miles away, I was concerned that Ziggy would make the move with me. His behavior was very disconcerting. And although medically he was in excellent health, emotionally he was very distraught. I hired Cat Whisperer, Mieshelle Nagelschneider. After a few appointments, Ziggy was ready for our thousand mile move from the Philadelphia suburbs to Melbourne, Florida. I became very chatty with Ziggy, telling him everything we were doing, and he would acknowledge in his various cat tones. He was telling me he was ready for the move.

About a month before we moved, I set up a Facebook page and posted pictures, quotes and cat videos of Ziggy and other cats. It became Ziggy's page or better known on Facebook as "Ziggy's Secrets" (or type into your browser www.Facebook.com/MyCoolCatZiggy). I made it fun and always wrote in his voice. He still demonstrates that he is a good sport through all the online attention. Within a year, we had over 2,000 followers.

Ziggy was more than willing to make the move and join me in our new home on the Space Coast of Florida. The morning we departed, he hopped into his traveling carrier willingly. Something I thought would be a challenge for both of us, along with the concern of adding fear to him for a long 2 day drive. I kept talking to him and still do, since I know he understands everything I say. I just wished I understood everything he says.

Shortly after we arrived at our new home and settled in, I set up a website for Ziggy (and my other felines that I've shared life with over the years). Because Ziggy coined the phrase "Thank God I'm a Feline" on his Facebook page (because every day is a TGIF day), I set up his URL as www.ThankGodImaFeline.com. It's a website totally devoted to the felines that have shared my life and a place to learn more about the other cat books I write. There is also the URL called MyCoolCatZiggy.com which funnels into his TGIF website: ThankGodImaFeline.com.

At age 11, Ziggy lives the life of a well nourished and extremely loved cat, living the good life of daily sunshine and constantly warm breezes. He's adjusted to life in Florida extremely well. He missed Zack for months after he was gone, but once we moved, he knew our new home was his and his alone. On occasion, I swear Zack's little spirit visits, because Ziggy makes the same cries of play when Zack was alive and they would romp around late at night. Ziggy continues to be a good sport with all the online postings, but continues to be aloof to visitors - even those that are dedicated cat lovers. Not to worry though, he's just keeping up his image of being My Cool Cat Ziggy!

Ziggy with the author's sandles

ABOUT THE AUTHOR

Rosemary Augustine

A native of Southern New Jersey, Rosemary Augustine spent most of her adult life living in Colorado and returned to the Philadelphia area in 2001 to care for an aging parent.

When Rosemary relocated from her home in Denver to the New Jersey / Pennsylvania area, something different happened besides a change of address. Rosemary embraced the culture of the northeast with a flair for creativity which opened a new direction for her as an artist and writer.

Rosemary calls herself a Journal Aficionado – her License Plate reads: "Journal" … and she offers many creative workshops focused on art-filled play and creative writing taking your spirit to new levels. Her artistic endeavors include acrylic and watercolor painting, designing and developing hand-crafted journals as well as a daily writing practice.

Rosemary has authored numerous books including *365 Days of Creative Writing* offering journal prompts for every day of the year. Her other books include: *Facing Changes In Employment*; *How To Live & Work Your Passion*; *Journal to a More Creative Self*; *Adventures with Byron*; *Ziggy's Secrets*; *Jenny's Secrets*; *Bucket List Journal*; *29 Things To Do*; *and I love My Job*.

Prior to 1991, Rosemary spent 20 years working in Corporate America and another 20 years helping people transition out of Corporate America. During her days in Corporate, she hired, managed and trained individuals. She worked for such companies as Integrated Resources, The Coach Store, Prudential Insurance and Twentieth Century-Fox Film Corporation. Beginning in 1980, she spent 10 years in the financial services industry, holding a NASD Series 7 Stock Broker's License and later worked as Director of Investor Relations for a Denver firm.

Rosemary is the owner of Blue Spruce Publishing and began her writing and publishing business in 1991 in Denver, Colorado. Today, she operates her life from a 2nd story condo in Melbourne, Florida, and shares her home with a feisty feline named

Ziggy, who is an inspiration for her art and writing. Along with his kitty brother Zack, both were an inspiration for this book.

Visit her online at: www.RosemaryAugustine.com; and visit Ziggy on Facebook at Ziggy's Secrets or at his website: www.ThankGodImaFeline.com.

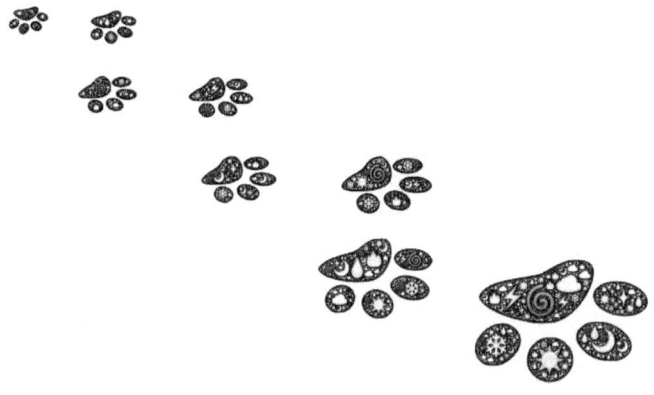

Rosemary Augustine

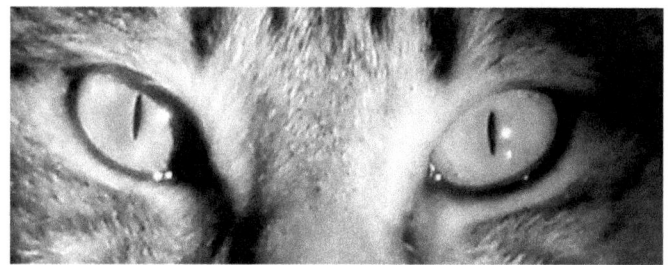

www.ingramcontent.com/pod-product-compliance
Lightning Source LLC
Chambersburg PA
CBHW071723040426
42446CB00011B/2197